WHY Did dinosaur skulls have windows?

Om KIDZ
An imprint of Om Books International

Contents

Why do dinosaurs usually have 'saur' in their name?

Saur means 'a lizard'! Dinosaurs were huge animals that lived millions of years ago. We get to know about dinosaurs by studying their fossils. When dinosaur fossils were first discovered by Robert Owen, he used the word dinosaur by combining the Greek words deinos, which means `terrible,' and sauros, which means `lizard'. Dinosaurs were thought to be gigantic versions of lizards, hence the use of 'saur' in their name.

Pocket fact

Spiky tail!
The thagomizer is an arrangement of spikes at the end of a dinosaur's tail. The term was coined by Gary Larson in a 1982 Far Side comic.

Why do palaeontologists dig dinosaur bones?

To find out more about dinosaurs! Palaeontologists are scientists who study fossils, that is the bones and remains of animals that were buried long ago. They keep careful records of the fossils they find and use this information later to identify the different types of dinosaurs and their habitats. By studying fossils, palaeontologists also get to know how things change under certain conditions and this helps them understand the relative magnitude of changes happening in today's world.

Find out

Take some play dough and make a dinosaur model of your own. What would you like to name your dinosaur?

Why was Tyrannosaurus Rex different from the other dinosaurs?

It had the strongest bite! Tyrannosaurus Rex was one of the largest meat-eating dinosaurs that ever lived. Its name means "the king of the tyrant lizards". This meat-eater was about 40 feet long and around 15–20 feet tall. It had a huge head with large, pointed, replaceable teeth and well-developed jaw muscles. Apart from its size, what made this dinosaur different from the others was its bite. Its bite could exert a force of up to 12,814 pounds, which is roughly equivalent to the force of a medium-sized elephant sitting down!

Find out

Which dinosaur had a spike on each hand?

Pocket fact

What a bite!
T. Rex is said to have had the most powerful bite of all! Its jaw exerted a crushing 3.6 tonnes of force, equivalent to the weight of three mid-sized cars.

Why did T. Rex leave small footprints although its feet were much longer?

Because it walked on its toes! Tyrannosaurus Rex, the huge meat-eating dinosaur lived about 85–65 million years ago. It had puny arms, but its feet were more impressive—almost 3.3 feet long. However, the T. Rex left only 1.55 feet-long footprints (even though its feet were much longer) because unlike humans, the T. Rex's heels did not touch the ground while walking!

Why does Stegosaurus have plates on its back?

To regulate heat! Stegosaurus was a large, plant-eating dinosaur that lived during the late Jurassic Period, about 150.8–155.7 million years ago. The most impressive features of the Stegosaurus were the two rows of bony plates, called scutes, along its back. The Stegosaurus' plates were embedded with a network of blood vessels and were probably used to regulate its body heat. It is believed that these plates would absorb light from the Sun during the day and dissipate extra body heat at night, thus controlling the Stegosaurus' body temperature.

Pocket fact

A lump in the tail!
The dinosaur Euoplocephalus had a tail with a bony lump. It swung its tail to hit its enemy with such a great force that it could break its bones!

Try this!

Work in pairs. Act as a Troodon and ask your friend to act as its prey. Play hide and seek. What senses did you use to hunt for your prey?

Why was Troodon also known as 'Wounding Teeth'?

Because of its saw-like teeth! Troodon was a small bird-like dinosaur from the Cretaceous period. The dinosaur was named so by palaeontologist Joseph Leidy who discovered a single serrated tooth belonging to it in Montana during the 1850s. The Troodon's teeth were different from those of most other theropods, as they bore prominent apically oriented serrations. These "wounding" serrations suggest that the dinosaur had a possibly omnivorous diet; and hence it got the name "wounding Tooth".

Find out

What did the Spinosaurus eat?

Why was the Diplodocus also called 'Old Whip-Tail'?

Because it had a whip-like tail! Diplodocus was a long-necked dinosaur, about 90-feet long with a whip-like tail that was 45-feet long. Diplodocus is also known as 'Old Whip-Tail' because it could swish its tail so hard that it made a crack like a whip! This would scare off its enemies.

Pocket fact

I am a big baby!

Newly hatched Diplodocus babies only weigh a few kilograms. However, they grow by one ton a year until they are adults. That's an astonishing 2–3 kilograms a day! By the time they are one-year-old, they measure almost 3 meters long and weigh as much as a full-grown horse.

Why do scientists say that the Spinosaurus lived in water?

It had some features that support aquatic life! The Spinosaurus was a large meat-eating dinosaur with a long sail on its back. It is the only known dinosaur that is said to have dwelled in water. Its nostrils were further up on its snout compared to that of the other dinosaurs. This would have allowed it to breathe even with most of its snout submerged in water. It had crocodile-like teeth that were ideal for catching fish. It also had paddle-like webbed feet that would've allowed the dinosaur to swim.

Why were Velociraptors compared to birds?

Because they had a lot in common with birds! Velociraptor was covered with feathers, had hollow bones, wishbones and also brooded their nests just like birds. Velociraptors also had quill knobs—places where the quills of the wing feathers of modern birds are anchored to the bone. If Velociraptors were alive today they would be considered as very unusual looking birds.

Pocket fact

Tiny raptor!

Microraptor gui, was one of the first raptor dinosaurs. It was less than two feet long and was covered in feathers.

Try this!

If you had to give some additional features to the Deinonychus, what would they be. Draw a picture to show these special features.

Why were Deinonychus's claws special?

Because of retracting talons! Deinonychus was a raptor with terrible claws—hence its name. It had three claws on its forelimbs and a large talon on its hind limbs. The dinosaur could retract the talons on its hind limbs, so that it could tuck them in for running and walking. Then it could bring them out again later to tear apart food.

Why didn't Sauropods walk on two legs?

Because they were heavy-weight! Sauropods were the largest animals to have ever lived on land. They were herbivores, and were usually quadrupeds, that is, they walked on four legs. They had small heads with large, massive bodies and long, counter-balancing tails. Due to their gigantic size, the Sauropods had thick legs to support their weight, with blunt, balanced feet that had five toes.

> **Pocket fact**
>
> **First discovered**
>
> The Corythosaurus was a plant-eating dinosaur and its fossil was first discovered in 1911 by Barnum Brown near Red Deer River located in Alberta, Canada.

> **Find out**
>
> How fast could Sauropods walk and run?

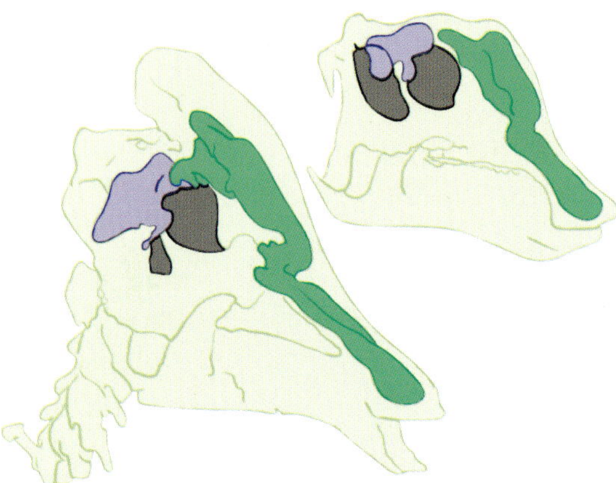

Why did the Corythosaurus wear a helmet?

Corythosaurus was a duck-billed dinosaur with a hollow, bony crest, shaped like a helmet on top of its long head. The dinosaur may have used it to make sounds, as a cooling device or for courtship displays. Corythosaurus' olfactory lobes, the part of the brain that senses smell, were located within the crest. So, it is likely that the crest must have been used as a sense-of-smell enhancer. Males had larger crests than females and juveniles.

Why is the Struthiomimus called an ostrich mimic?

The Struthiomimus was a light-weight member of the pre-historic dinosaur world. It was medium sized, light in build and had a long neck. It also had long rear limbs that appeared to be suitable for great speed and distance coverage, like that of an ostrich. It was similar to the ostrich in terms of its strength, its nimble nature and even its likely feathers. Hence, it was named the Struthiomimus.

Pocket fact

We are the noisiest!
The Parasaurolophus were probably the noisiest of all dinosaurs. It is assumed that they might have made a bellowing sound, like a giant trumpet!

Try this!

Can you name any three dinosaurs that were similar to an ostrich?

Why did Parasaurolophus have a crest on its head?

The Parasaurolophus belonged to the Hadrosaurs group of dinosaurs that were known for their strange head ornaments. It had a long, narrow, backward-curving crest that grew out of the back of its skull. The crest had long distinct tubes. Scientists believe that the two hollow tubes inside the crest might have been used to make distinctive sounds, distinctive enough to have been identified individually, so that they could call and communicate with others in their herd.

Why were some meat-eating dinosaurs called Raptors?

They were fast-moving dinosaurs similar to birds! Raptor fossils have been found all over the world, including China, the United States and Argentina. They were slim, clever and fast dinosaurs with their bodies covered in feathers. In addition to feathers, they had a special, long-toe claw which was used to hold onto and kill the prey. Raptors also had flexible forearms that they used for grabbing.

Try this!

When did hadrosaurs live on Earth?

Pocket fact

The first raptor dinosaurs appeared over 120 million years ago. *Microraptor gui*, as its name implies, was a tiny dinosaur, less than two feet long. It was covered in feathers and is considered the most bird-like dinosaur.

Why were some dinosaurs grouped as hadrosaurs?

They had many similar characteristics! 'Hadrosaurs' were plant-eating dinosaurs that mostly moved about on two legs, although the larger species probably walked on all fours. They were dinosaurs with a horny beak for picking-off plants and very effective teeth for chewing. Hadrosaurs had massive and inflexible tails, tough beaks and numerous cheek teeth. Their thick torsos gave them the name hadrosaurs which means bulky lizard.

Why is the Oviraptor also called the 'egg hunter'?

It was thought to hunt eggs! The Oviraptor was a meat-eating dinosaur from the late Cretaceous period. In 1922, James B. Shackleford discovered the fossil of a plant-eating dinosaur called Protoceratops. Later, in 1924, a technician named George Olsen discovered a nest of dinosaur eggs near the same place and it was assumed that the eggs belonged to the Protoceratops. However, the dinosaur fossil found near this nest belonged to an Oviraptor, which led to the assumption that the Oviraptor was trying to steal the Protoceratops' eggs. This is how the Oviraptor earned its name "egg hunter". However, years later it was found that the eggs belonged to the Oviraptor itself and the dinosaur was only trying to protect its own eggs.

Find out

The Ankylosaurus's skin was covered with Osteoderms. What are Osteoderms?

Pocket fact

We care!

Some dinosaurs looked after their babies until they were old enough to take care of themselves. One such dinosaur was the Maiasaura that fed its babies and protected them too.

Why was it difficult to attack the Ankylosaurs?

Because it was the largest of all armoured dinosaurs! The Ankylosaurus lived about 70-65 million years ago. It had thick bony plates all over its body. Its head was also covered with plates and spikes. It even had bony plates around its eyelids! The dinosaur also had a bony club at the end of its tail. Such heavy armour made it difficult for other dinosaurs to attack the Ankylosaurus.

Why didn't some dinosaurs chew their food?

Because they didn't have molars! Palaeontologists have discovered that huge plant-eating dinosaurs did not chew their food but just gulped it. These dinosaurs had a grinding organ called a gizzard, just like birds, alligators and seals do. They would swallow stones as big as softballs. When they swallowed food, the rocks helped to mash the food up, turning it into pulp.

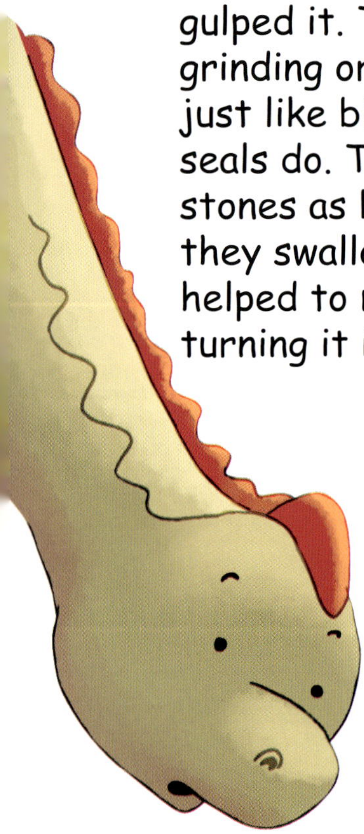

Find out

How big is a dinosaur tooth?

Pocket fact

We have gizzards too!

The grinding organ called gizzard is also found in the digestive tract of some present-day animals, including crocodiles, alligators, earthworms and even birds.

Why did the teeth of the Dilophosaurus break-off easily?

Because its jawbones were not strongly connected! The Dilophosaurus had several odd features, such as its jawbones were not strongly connected, it had a gap behind its forward teeth and its teeth also had a narrow base. This could have been the reason why its teeth might have broken-off more easily, while feeding, compared to the teeth of the other big meat eaters. Some scientists think that with all of these features, the Dilophosaurus could only have eaten fish or already dead animals.

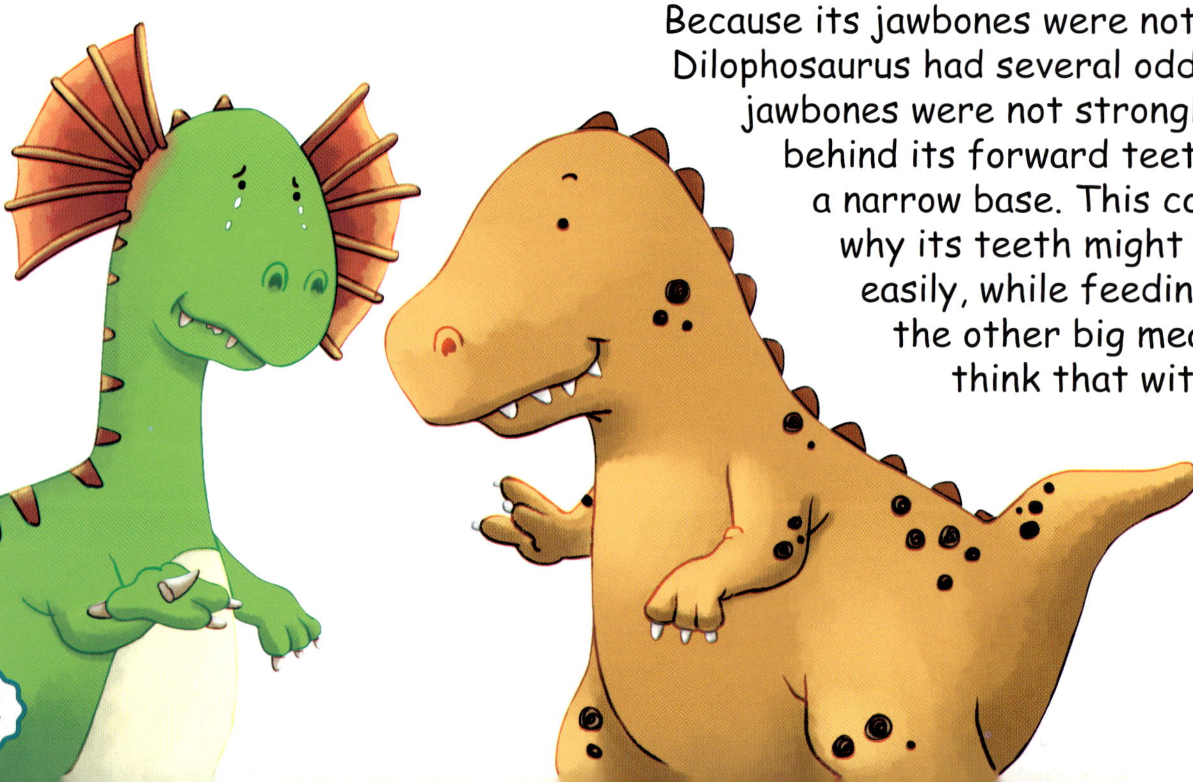

Why did Euoplocephalus's eyes have bony shutters?

To protect itself from enemies! Euoplocephalus was a heavily-armoured dinosaur that lived in North America about 75 million years ago. It was covered with bony plates from head to tail. Its eyes were protected by armour. Each eyelid was actually a small, round bone that closed like a shutter when the dinosaur was attacked!

Find out

Which dinosaur had a beak-shaped mouth without teeth?

Pocket fact

What's my name!

Euoplocephalus was discovered by Lawrence Lambe in 1902. He proposed the name "Stereocephalus". However, the name "Stereocephalus" was already being used for an insect. Hence, the dinosaur was named Euoplocephalus in 1910.

Why did Sauropelta have both teeth and beak?

To gather low-growing plants and chew them! Sauropelta was an armoured dinosaur from the Cretaceous period. It looked a lot like the Ankylosaurus, but did not have a bony tail and horns on its head. Sauropelta had a narrow skull with big jaws and small, leaf-shaped cheek teeth. However, it did not have any front teeth but had a toothless horny beak. It used the beak to gather foliage and the small cheek teeth to mash them.

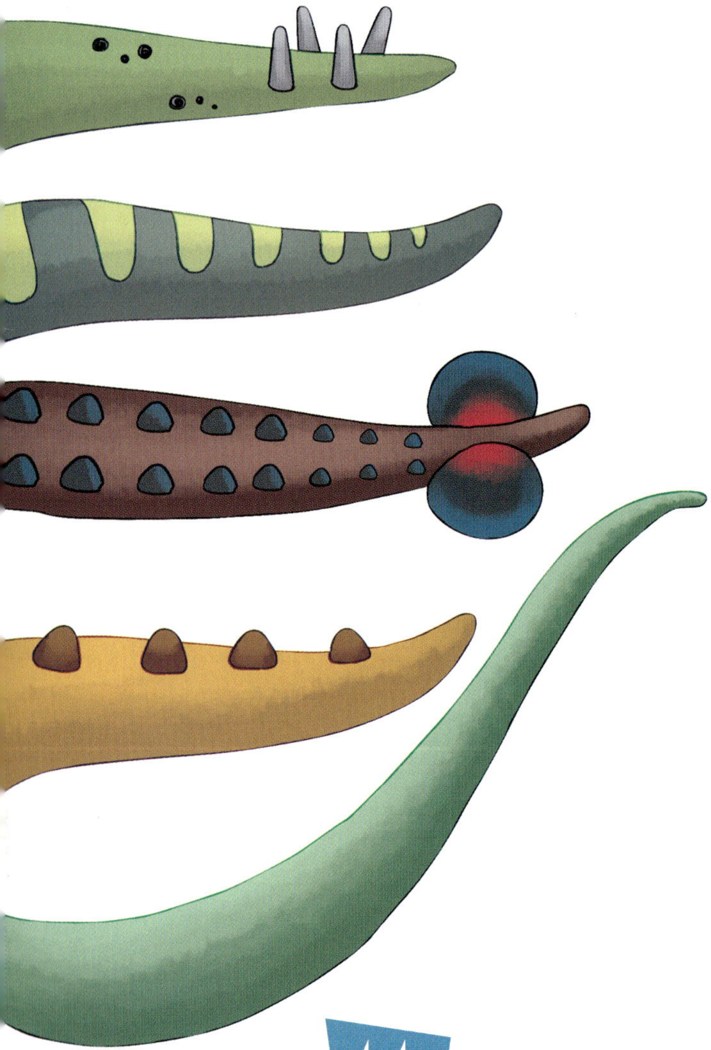

Why did dinosaurs have tails?

It served them several purposes! Most dinosaurs had large tails that had different uses. The tails of most dinosaurs helped them counterbalance their long neck or large, heavy head. The tails of fast-running dinosaurs helped them balance swift turns while running. Some dinosaurs like the Ankylosaurus had bony tails which they used for defense. And Sauropods had long whip-like tails that not only balanced their heavy body but also helped them scare away their enemies!

Find out

Which dinosaurs had holes in their jaws?

Pocket fact

That's the idea!
The idea that some Sauropods may have used their massive tails as a whip to lash at their attackers was given by the British zoologist R. McNeill Alexander in 1961.

Why did dinosaur skulls have windows?

To reduce the weight of the skull! Dinosaurs had holes in their skulls called "fenestrae," which means "windows" or "openings" in Latin. The ones located in the back portion of the skull were for the expansion of jaw muscles. The ones in front of the eye and sides were probably for lightening the skull, or for heat-loss purposes.

Why did T. Rex have small arms?

Because it didn't use them for hunting or walking! Most dinosaurs used their arms to walk or to hunt their prey. T. Rex, the king of dinosaurs, had small arms as compared to its body size. It was 42-feet long and weighed 7–9 tons. It walked on its hind limbs. It had a long tail that had over 40 bones, which helped balance the animals' huge head. It had 4-feet-long jaws filled with 50–60 sharp teeth. Its conical and serrated teeth were able to grab 500 pounds of meat in a single bite.

Try this!

Use an egg carton and a cupcake liner to make a model of the Triceratops. Use the carton for the face and the cupcake liner as a frill behind the Triceratops' head.

Pocket fact

Extremely powerful!
Even though the T. Rex's arms were small as compared to its body but they were quite strong. It's believed that the T. Rex may have been capable of lifting approximately 450 pounds in each arm.

Why did the Triceratops wear a frill around its neck?

It had several functions! Triceratops was a large herbivore from the Late Cretaceous period. It had a big, bony frill extending from the back of its skull and covering its neck. The elaborate frill may have been used as armour to protect itself from its predators. The frill also had spikes that could have been used in the displays of rivals competing for territory or to attract mates.

Index